D0284487

FRENCH IMPRESSIONISTS

Paintings

To Don, with thoughts of love.

WINGS BOOKS

New York • Avenel, New Jersey

*uncle Paul
our amit.*

1996.

Copyright © 1994 by Random House Value Publishing, Inc.

This 1994 edition is published by Wings Books,
distributed by Random House Value Publishing, Inc.,
40 Engelhard Avenue, Avenel, New Jersey 07001.

Grateful acknowledgment is made to Art Resource for permission to use their
transparencies of the artwork.

Random House
New York • Toronto • London • Sydney • Auckland

Printed and bound in Malaysia

Library of Congress Cataloging-in-Publication Data

French Impressionists : paintings.
     p.   cm.
   Includes bibliographical references.
   ISBN 0-517-11924-2
   1. Impressionism (Art)—France.   2. Post-impressionism (Art)—
France.
ND547.5.I4F74   1994
759.4'09'034—dc20   94-20389
                                         CIP

8   7   6   5   4   3   2

"When you go out to paint, try to forget what objects you have before you; a tree, a house, a field. . . . Merely think here is a little square of blue, here an oblong of pink, here a streak of yellow, and paint it just as it looks to you, the exact colour and shape, until it gives you your own naive impression of the scene before you." [1]

—CLAUDE MONET

1. EDOUARD MANET
    Luncheon on the Grass (*Le Déjeuner sur l'herbe*)   1863

2. EDOUARD MANET
Sunday on the Seine (Argenteuil) 1874

3. EDOUARD MANET
   On the Beach 1873

4.   EDOUARD MANET
     Bar at the Folies-Bergère
     1881–82

5. CLAUDE MONET
Rouen Cathedral, Harmony in Blue and Gold,
Full Sunshine 1894

6. CLAUDE MONET
Impression, Sunrise 1872

7. CLAUDE MONET
Luncheon on the Grass 1866

8. CLAUDE MONET
La rue Montorgueil,   June 30, 1878

9. CLAUDE MONET
The Water Lily Pond, Pink Harmony   1900

10. CLAUDE MONET
     Regatta at Argenteuil   1872

11.   CAMILLE PISSARRO
Approach to the Village   1872

12. CAMILLE PISSARRO
Red Roofs   1877

13. CAMILLE PISSARRO
The Seine River and the Louvre

14. **PIERRE-AUGUSTE RENOIR**
Young Girls at the Piano   1892

15. **PIERRE-AUGUSTE RENOIR**
    Claude Renoir as a Clown   1909

16. **PIERRE-AUGUSTE RENOIR**
Woman with a Fan   1881

17. PIERRE-AUGUSTE RENOIR
The Swing 1876

18. **PIERRE-AUGUSTE RENOIR**
Le Moulin de la Galette 1876

19.   EDGAR DEGAS
       Race Horses Before the Stands   C. 1879

20.   EDGAR DEGAS
      Dancer with Bouquet, Bowing   C. 1877

21. EDGAR DEGAS
Blue Dancers C. 1890

22. EDGAR DEGAS
End of the Arabesque

23. PAUL CÉZANNE
Still Life with Peaches and Pears c. 1888–90

24. PAUL CÉZANNE
Mont Sainte-Victoire C. 1900

25. PAUL CÉZANNE
    The Card Players   1892

26. VINCENT VAN GOGH
    The Siesta, after Millet   1889–90

27.   VINCENT VAN GOGH
      The Sower   1888

28. Vincent van Gogh
The Artist's Bedroom at Arles   1889

Afterword

In 1863, a young artist from the French patrician class presented a new work at the Salon des Refusés, an exhibition of paintings that had been rejected by the official Salon of Paris. The artist was Edouard Manet. The painting was *Le Déjeuner sur l'herbe* (plate 1), a contemporary picnic scene in the countryside outside Paris that outraged the public and critics alike. More enlightened critics recognized that Manet was engaged in something revolutionary. Manet ignored the old rules about what a painting should *be*—nonambiguous, composed around a historical, religious, or classical theme; and what a painting should *do*—narrate or interpret events, uplift and inspire the viewer. Manet simply painted what he saw before him—in *Le Déjeuner*, modern men and women relaxing in a simple landscape imbued with light and color—and invited the viewer to *see* along with him.

This was a sight that demanded new sensibilities. The female nude is not presented in classical or mythological terms, but naturally, at ease in her world. Manet's use of color and light is also markedly different from that of the old masters. In classical works, "light and color were subservient to the meaning of the painting and the individuality of the artist was kept in check. Such pictures demanded a high finish built on accurate drawing, controlled brushwork, controlled gradation of tones and a limited range of colors."[2] Manet's technique is instead characterized by a vibrant and almost frenetic handling of brush and pigment, so that "the flow of the brushstrokes evokes physical sensations, an immediate shift between light and dark with the elimination of half-tones, a purity of colour and an exploitation of contrasts."[3]

Le Déjeuner sur l'herbe may arguably be viewed as a door between conservative, academically-based schools of painting and a new generation of painters who had been looking for a more truthful and personal view of the world. *Le Déjeuner* and Manet's equally controversial *Olympia*, painted in the same year, challenged painters of the mid- and late-1860s to reexamine the past and celebrate contemporary themes with innovative uses of light, color, and composition.

This challenge was taken up by a group of artists who would not achieve their greatest recognition for nearly another decade. In 1863, as they painted and exhibited their first works, Manet became a hero and leader to the pioneers of Impressionism. He provided them a new venue from which to see and capture on canvas a radically changed Paris, whose streets and boulevards had been redesigned to open the city to light and air, and whose emerging middle class—freed by industrialization and modernized transportation—pursued the lifestyles of leisure, entertainment, and travel.

Each of the greatest Impressionists—Claude Monet, Camille Pissaro, Pierre-Auguste Renoir, Edgar Degas, Paul Cézanne, and Vincent van Gogh—would uniquely explore and master themes and techniques introduced by Manet: the vagaries of light, color, and motion; city nights and country days; the intricate variations of the human form at rest and play.

The first Impressionist exhibition, presented at the *Société anonyme* in 1874, displayed works of Monet, Pissarro, Renoir, Degas, and Cézanne. The exhibition was generally ill-received but Monet's *Impression, Sunrise* (plate 6) was targeted for some particularly derisive comments by the critic and satirist Louis Leroy:

> *Impression*—I was sure of it. I was just telling myself that, since I was impressed, there had to be some impression in it . . . and what freedom, what ease of workmanship! Wallpaper in its embryonic state is more finished than this seascape.[4]

Leroy's comments gave birth to both the name of the group and their style of painting, a label with which none of them were comfortable: they never espoused any formal "manifesto" or saw themselves as a unified group. This was, in fact, the first and last time they would all exhibit together in one show. While they shared a similar commitment to exploring new uses of color and subject matter, each was pursuing a distinctive style of his own.

In the 1870s and early 1880s, Monet, Renoir, and Pissarro became perhaps the most influential of the "open-air" impressionists, inspiring one critic to conclude that, "they render not the landscape, but the sensation produced by the landscape."[5] Monet and Renoir, who had been students together at Charles Gleyre's famous studio (often called the "nursery of Impressionism"), and later spent a summer together painting at Argenteuil, produced luminous suburban impressions of river, countryside, and people at play. These paintings are often centered around one dominant theme and have an almost energetic quality, rendered with quick brushstrokes, bright color and light, and applications of pure pigment. Monet's *Regatta at Argenteuil* (plate 10) and Renoir's *Le Moulin de la Galette* (plate 18) and *The Swing* (plate 17) are characteristic of this period in the two painters' careers.

Edouard Manet also painted with Monet and Renoir at Argenteuil, and produced several canvases that clearly showed their influence. *Sunday on the Seine (Argenteuil)* (plate 2) and *On the Beach* (plate 3) are less stylized and controlled than Manet's early paintings, and are characterized by softer lines and warmer colors. Echoes of the Argenteuil paintings would later be seen in Manet's fully Impressionistic masterpiece, *Bar at the Folies-Bergère* (plate 4).

In marked contrast to the styles of Monet and Renoir, Camille Pissarro's impressionistic landscapes are decidely rural and evocative of ordinary country life. *Approach to the Village* (plate 11) and *Red Roofs* (plate 12) have a quietly deliberate quality to them, characterized by smooth, subtle brushstrokes and carefully blended colors.[6]

Monet, whose name would become synonymous with Impressionism, quickly struck out on his own and began a lifelong exploration of the myriad effects of light and color. He said of his own *Luncheon on the Grass* (plate 7)—a reworking of Manet's *Le Déjeuner* which Monet never completed—that it was his first attempt at experimenting with the division of color by light. Thirty years later, *Rouen Cathedral* (plate 5), one of a remarkable series of paintings, was a masterful testament to the power of the shifting qualities of light. Here, form and color, blues and golds, coalesce until the object painted is "discredited," made abstract, by its renderings under different conditions, and by the artist's own response to it over time. The notion of the "discredited object" was one of the greatest contributions of Monet's series paintings, the most famous of which are the water-lily paintings done in the 1900s.[7]

Renoir also left the Impressionist group, and concentrated on the official Salon of Paris as an outlet for his work. Drawing on his early roots as a porcelain painter, his extensive knowledge of the masters, and the techniques he had begun to explore with Monet, Renoir returned to painting the human form in a new manner. His technique became softer, more classical, with a subtler use of light and delicate applications of warmer colors. The luminous quality achieved in *Young Girls at the Piano* (plate 14) is characteristic of his post-Impressionist period. Using a limited palette to explore the pure power of color, Renoir declared, "I want a red to be sonorous, to sound like a bell," and *Claude Renoir as a Clown* (plate 15) is indeed a celebration of reds—an effect fully intended by the painter.[8] By the end of his career, Renoir, of all the Impressionists, was considered the most brilliant in his use of color.

Edgar Degas, the youngest of the group and the only one to exhibit in all eight of the Impressionist exhibitions (from 1874 to 1886), was distinguished from his fellow Impressionists by an almost obsessive preference for painting people rather than landscapes and for rejecting their explorations of color in favor of mastering his already considerable drawing techniques. Throughout his career he would celebrate contemporary culture through paintings of the ballet, opera, cafe, circus, horse races, and brothels. He was especially drawn to the nuances of physical motion, particularly the subtle movements caught "in the moment" before and after an event. *Race Horses Before the Stands* (plate 19), *Dancer with Bouquet, Bowing* (plate 20), and *End of the Arabesque* (plate 22) are all characterized by his "urge to capture the fleeting movement."[9] Though Degas had a deep affinity for the past, his reinterpretation of it in modern terms was every bit as radical as Manet's had been. Like Manet, Degas revolutionized the female form. About Degas's paintings of modern women, one critic noted:

> There is certainly a woman there, but a certain kind of woman, without the expression of a face . . . a woman reduced to the gesticulation of her limbs, to the appearance of her body, a woman considered as a female, expressed in her animality.[10]

Aspects of Degas's "new woman," who would be rendered in almost abstract terms by the end of his career, can be seen in *Blue Dancers* (plate 21).

Paul Cézanne, the father of Modernism, and Vincent van Gogh, who would contribute much to the Symbolists, are generally viewed as post- or neo-Impressionists. Cézanne painted with the Impressionist group for only six years (1873–1879), where he was greatly influenced by the works and teachings of Pissarro. Van Gogh did not arrive in Paris until the late 1880s, near the end of the "Impressionist Decade." Both painters applied their considerable talents and unique, personal perspectives to reworking some of the fundamental precepts of Impressionism. In doing so, each created a new artistic consciousness and laid the groundwork for what would become Modern art.

When Cézanne said of Monet, that he was "only any eye—but what an eye!", this was, at once, a compliment and a call to arms. While Cézanne acknowledged Impressionism's great achievement in forcing the viewer to *see* "the fugitive and the contingent in human experience," he was also saying that "seeing" was no longer enough.[11] He believed that what is felt and known about a subject, whether landscape, still life, or human figure, is equally important. Cézanne wanted to make a "more solid and enduring" art that went beyond exploring the effects of light and color. "I paint what I see and how I feel," he said. With a stroke, he eliminated "traditional spatial notions of foreground, background, and depth" and literally reconstructed nature.[12] Cézanne's call for a "fundamental reordering of experience" would later be echoed in Cubist works and can already be seen in his *Still Life with Peaches and Pears* (plate 23), *Mont Sainte-Victoire* (plate 24), and *The Card Players* (plate 25), all of which are now recognized as early Modernist works.

It was left to Vincent van Gogh to go beyond the "seen and felt." As Pissarro would tellingly remark, "This man would either go mad or outpace us all. That he would do both I did not foresee."

Painting in Holland, Van Gogh's first works were somber, monochromatic, and oppressingly realistic—*The Potato Eaters,* a dark study of the peasant working class, is typical of this period. He further explored his affinity with the working classes after arriving in France, when he saw the works of Jean-François Millet, the renowned painter of the French peasantry, who Van Gogh would idolize and emulate all his life.[13]

The Siesta, after Millet (plate 26) and *The Sower* (plate 27) are Van Gogh's homages to Millet's "truth and simplicity." Van Gogh also embraced the liberating qualities extolled by the Impressionists. He expanded upon their use of pure color and quick brushwork to such a personally explosive degree that his later works approach a mystical and symbolic quality that is often inexplicable: the meaning of *Starry Night* (back cover), for example, has forever remained a mystery. His early French paintings of more traditional subjects, works like *Green Vase of Flowers* (title page), and later *The Artist's Bedroom at Arles* (plate 28), have a newly passionate air about them. Here are the beginnings of Van Gogh's attempts to use color and line expressly to paint that which is emotional and personal. This is art not just seen, not just felt, but wholly experiential: the art *and* the artist are equally revealed.

The Impressionist's invitation to see, to feel, and ultimately, to experience an art reborn, was met with grudging reluctance by their conservative peers but was joyously celebrated by later generations.

Perhaps it is enough to say that having seen the sunlight bathe Rouen Cathedral, dapple the grass at Argenteuil, or filter through a tiny bedroom window in Arles, we see such things ever after as Monet and Renoir and Van Gogh saw them.[14]

NOTES

1. Robert Katz and Celestine Dars, *The Impressionists in Context* (New York: Crescent Books), 94
2. Ibid, 13
3. Ibid, 13
4. Ibid, 20
5. Ibid, 106
6. *Impressionism and European Modernisms: The Sirak Collection* (Columbus Museum of Art, Ohio), 14
7. Katz and Dars, 224
8. Patrick Bade, *Renoir: The Masterworks* (New York: Portland House), 30
9. Katz and Dars, 196
10. Ibid, 194
11. John Russell, *The Meanings of Modern Art, Volume 1* (The Museum of Modern Art, New York), 13
12. Katz and Dars, 318–319
13. Richard Muhlberger, *What Makes A Van Gogh A Van Gogh?* (New York: The Metropolitan Museum of Art and Viking), 40
14. Russell, 13

List of Plates

All the photographs of the paintings reproduced in this book were supplied by Art Resource, New York: